For Men

Helping Men Prepare For Life's Battles

24 Week Bible Study For Men

Rex Tignor

With

Mark Allen, Jack Eaton, David Garrett,

Dan Lapham, Matt Long, Callis West

© **Copyright**
Permission to make handouts for each group member
Copyright © Rex Tignor
All rights reserved.

ISBN: 1523424109
ISBN 13: 9781523424108

BOOT CAMP

In this book, you will find 24 weeks of lesson outlines. Please feel free to make a copy of each week, adding your thoughts and your life to each point make it your own.

We only covered each topic for one week on purpose; we paid attention to the ones that hit men pretty hard. After the 24 weeks, the men were asked would they like to spend additional sessions talking about these topics in depth. Next thing you know, it's been a year, and you will find you truly have a group of brothers.

2 Keys

1. Ask this question at the end of ever session: What is one thing you are taking out of here tonight you will apply in your life?

2. Open and close in Prayer: Keep it short and simple model prayer is just simply talking to God.

The Men On The Cover

The men on the cover with me are men that have spent four years in Boot Camp learning how to lead and pour their lives into other men that attend the next round of Boot Camp. They are now teaching these lessons in their own groups.

I can tell you that these men on the cover with me have my back for anything, even at 2 a.m.

Let me ask you: Who has your back, and whose back do you have?

If you have any questions or we can help in any way, please feel free to contact us. Our e-mail information is under "About The Authors."

TABLE OF CONTENTS

Meet The Authors vi

Boot Camp For Men Book viii

Start Up Kit For Boot Camp Groups x

Accountability Questions For Men xii

Week 1 A True Friend Moving From Facebook to FaceTime 2

Week 2 A Real Man 4

Week 3 Letting Go of The Past God Loves Do-Overs 6

Week 4 Storms 8

Week 5 What If I Took Control of My Words? 10

Week 6 Conflict 12

Week 7 Anger 14

Week 8 Forgiveness 16

Week 9 Anxiety and Stress 18

Week 10 Decisions 20

Week 11 The Path to A Fall 22

Week 12 Don't Let The Enemy Loot Your Life 24

Week 13 Your Wife Needs A Hero - And It's You 26

Week 14 7 Tips for Communication In Marriage 28

Week 15 Children 30

Week 16	Work	32
Week 17	It's Your Time	34
Week 18	Unpacking Your Lunch	36
Week 19	Discovering Your Purpose	38
Week 20	Discovering Your Purpose	40
Week 21	God's NOW Moments	42
Week 22	Living to Leave a Legacy	44

2 Special Weeks

Week - Before Christmas
What Kind of Man Was Joseph?..46

Week - After Christmas Break
Telling Your Story..47

Extra Sessions..49

Prayer Made Simple..51

A Daily Quiet Time or Bible Study..52

MEET THE AUTHORS

Rex Tignor

Boot Camp is something God put on my heart. I had men coming up to me asking me to start a group for men that dealt with the issues men face. So I contacted Jack Eaton and casted the vision of Boot Camp, and he said "let's do it"; so we did. The other men you see below are men that have grabbed a hold of this and are using it to impact the lives of other men. rex@manupministries.net

Mark Allen

These lessons did not come to me in a classroom. The 6 men on the front cover lived them in front of me. My life was wrecked when we met. Now, it's ordered and I live it with and in front of other men.

I prepare men for battle. Does your life prepare men for the battles? tmallen1223@gmail.com

Jack Eaton

Like most men I lived life on a day-to-day basis - same thing every day, just like the movie "Ground Hog Day". I would say, "I know the cards that life dealt me and that's just the way it's going to be." Then one day, God got my attention and I was brought to my knees. My friendship with Rex Tignor pushed me to use my past experiences to impact the lives of men. We decided to challenge men, and as seen in the summaries on this page, lives have been forever changed as a result. This guide is a great resource for a group of men to use, so dig in and start impacting your family in ways you have never dreamed of… and the journey begins. Jeaton6460@gmail.com

David Garrett
Why DO I Just Want to Show Up in Men's Lives?

Very few men ever showed up in my life as mentors and leaders unless I asked them. Even then, they may not have responded or did respond but the relationship lasted only shortly. It is especially interesting that I do not ever remember a Christian man showing up in my life or that of any of my friends.

As a relatively new Christian (I accepted Christ at the young age of 58), I have 30 more years of an open window to reach men and share with them. I do not want so much to share, "Men, do it this way and you will be a better man." I want to share what I and others of my generation have done poorly and to have the next generation not mess up.

"Showing up" means to show men that you want to breath life into them; not to take it out of them. Make them believe that they are significant to their families, friends and co-workers. Watch what happens when you tell a man you "**love**" him as a Christian brother, that you are "**proud**" of him and that he is "**good at**" a specific area of his life (what are his true gifts). I want to show up when it is not convenient. What a message this sends to a man's self worth.

Hopefully my son's generation will say of my generation, "They were there when we needed them. Let them know unconditional love from the true Father. www.menjustshowup.com - David-Garrett@msn.com

Dan Lapham

When I first started going to Boot Camp, I wasn't too sure what to expect. I have always been a person to keep my feelings and family business to myself. I always felt no one wants to hear about my past and I didn't want anyone to feel sorry for me, once they heard it. Through this group of men I have been able to open up more about the past and what is going on in my current life. Hearing other men's stories has made me realize I'm not the only one who stumbles through life. These men are closer than my biological brothers and will be there through any journey good or bad that I will travel in the future. d52lapham@gmail.com

Matt Long

I didn't realize I was in need of a boot camp until I was in the midst of a war. Some training on what to do and when to do it would have helped before ending up here. Unprepared, alone, and looking for answers but not even knowing the right questions to ask to even get out of the ruts I have created. Boot camp helped guide me to ask the right questions to others and myself for the truth. That's what I was in search of all this time: THE REAL TRUTH. Getting Godly men around me speaking truth and holding me accountable for my actions allowed me to become a better husband, father, and friend. It doesn't mean the storms won't come and life becomes easy. It means I have the tools today to get through the storms confidently knowing Gods truth. Longsbiz@yahoo.com

Callis West

God sought after my heart for many years to walk with other men. And, for many years I have run from that call choosing isolation instead. One summer night during a church prayer service in 2011, Rex Tignor followed God's command and found me. He spoke life into my situation and I have been walking with these men since that evening. callis.west@gmail.com

BOOT CAMP FOR MEN BOOK

The lessons in this book deal with issues that men face every day. You will see they are in week 1-24 order. All lessons are on two pages so you can copy them and use them as you see fit. You will also find the points you can use as you teach each lesson, and a place to add your own thoughts - you need to make it your own.

Here are our rules for Boot Camp. I know they are tough, but I have found if you call men to a challenge, the ones that really want to go to another level in their walk with God will go with you.

We average 15 men a session.

Boot Camp For Men

- We are asking for a 24-week Commitment

- Commit to 3 out of 4 weeks. If 3 weeks are missed in a row you will not be allowed back in this session.

- If something comes up (LIFE) and you must miss a night, CALL Rex or Jack - NO text or e-mail. This keeps down the "I had a rough day."

- If life happens and you need time away, you may sit down with the leaders to talk about it. We want to know how we can still support you.

- You must be willing to keep total confidentiality.

- You must lose your religious pat answers at the door. We will look at life and what the BIBLE has to say about it.

- You must read the assigned text for the following week and bring your Bible.

- We will start on time and finish on time. Doors <u>WILL</u> be shut from 7:02pm - 8:30pm

- Be willing to be held accountable and accept phone calls from other group members.

- You must be willing to sign an agreement to the above.

- In the event of bad weather, we will follow Henrico County Schools.

* I understand that if I break the rules above, I will be asked to leave the group.

START UP KIT FOR BOOT CAMP GROUPS

Start with a Few (Reach 3 to 7 Men)

1. Provide "safety"
You'll need to allow the men in your small group a lot of time for the walls to start coming down. This will be a gradual process. Your group needs to be a place where the trust level goes up, so that group members are willing to share their lives.

2. Keep Your Focus
Make sure from the start that you have decided as a group what your purpose is, and stick to it. It will be easy to slide into other things, topics and conversations.

3. <u>Start</u> and <u>Finish</u> on Time – <u>key</u>
One person in the group should have the responsibility to start the group on time and let everyone know when the committed time is up.

4. Focus on People, Not Programs
It will be easy to discuss lots of great subjects and to debate theological issues and never get to the matters of the heart. Start your group with plenty of time for the group members to get to know one another. Maybe schedule a night to just hang out. Relationships are key.

5. Be challenging
Most men are sick and tired of only talking about sports and the weather; they want to go deeper and be challenged. Men will extend themselves if they know what the goal is and what they will get out of it. They want to be involved in something significant and life-changing.

6. Move Slowly
Men do not easily reveal the hurts, pains and frustrations of their lives. It takes time, so move slowly. Before vulnerability will happen in your group, you will need to start by developing an environment of unconditional love and acceptance, not one of judgment. Build men up; do not beat them up.

7. Take the Lead
Most men will not share their fears, failures, or feelings because they don't know how and have never been in a safe environment to do so.
   Take the lead by example.

8. Life
Some of the greatest ministry will take place outside your sessions, when specific needs arise in the lives of the men in your group. Make yourselves available to help in those times of need and feel free to call the others in your group for help.

9. Take Men On A Journey
Help men define, discover and develop their God-given potential and raise their level of expectancy.

10. Discussion
There are three simple guidelines: wait your turn, stay on the topic, and keep it brief. *(post-it note)*

11. Small Group Prayer
The ABC's of small group prayer are: **Audible**, so all can hear; **Brief**, so that you do not take everyone else's time; and **Christ-centered**, so as not to spend all your time praying about uncle Jim's ingrown toenail. *If someone does not feel comfortable praying aloud, make sure he knows he does not have to.*

12. Multiply
Always be on the lookout for other leaders.

6 Known Killers of Small Groups ---Beware!
Aimlessness, Poor leadership, Controlled by the wrong one, Shallowness, Individualism, Competition.

Five "M's" to keep in mind

1. Minister to the men, not at them
2. Mentor their spiritual maturity
3. Motivate men to discover their God given potential
4. Model a surrendered heart
5. Multiply

Permission to use from: Group.com

ACCOUNTABILITY QUESTIONS FOR MEN

Go through the list below and pick out 5 Accountability Questions that fit your men. Challenge them to contact each other throughout the week.

When this starts to happen, you will see the group come together as brothers.

Accountability Questions for Men
Have you spent time with God on a regular basis?
Have you compromised your integrity in any way?
Has your thought life been pure?
Have you committed any sexual sin?
Did you put yourself in an awkward situation with a woman?
Anything plagued your walk with God this week?
Did you accomplish your spiritual goals this week?
How have you demonstrated a servant's heart?
Do you treat your peers and coworkers as people loved by God?
What significant thing did you do for your wife and/or family?
What was your biggest disappointment? How did you decide to handle it?
What was your biggest joy? Did you thank God?
What do you see as your number one need for next week?
Are you satisfied with the time you spent with God this week?
Did you take time to show compassion for others in need?
Did you control your tongue?
What did you do this week to enhance your relationship with your spouse and child(ren)?
Did you pray and read God's Word this week? What did you get from that time?
In what ways have you stepped out in faith since we last met?
Any disappointments consumed your thoughts this week?
How have you been tempted this week? How did you respond?
Did you worship in church this week?
What are you wrestling with in your thought life?
Are the "visible" you and the "real" you consistent?

These are my 3 favorite accountability questions for men to ask each other
1. What did you learn today?

2. What could you have done better today?

3. What would you change about today?

YOUR BOOTCAMP RULES

A TRUE FRIEND
MOVING FROM FACEBOOK TO FACETIME

Who is riding Shotgun in your life?
We have too many men getting picked off daily because they do not have that man that they can call when life hits hard.

Bible Study: Mark 2:1-5 and 11-12
Talk about 1 hurting man, 4 men coming along side of him willing to do whatever it took to get him to Jesus.

Talk about the qualities of a true friend
As they call out their word ask them in a few words to explain it.
    Allow the list to grow… (space is provided for your list)

Supports you
Listens to you
Encourages you

Now talk about the keys to being a true friend
Be Confidential - A faithful friend is one who doesn't share your life with others.
    Proverbs 11:13: "A gossip betrays a confidence, but a trustworthy man keeps a secret."
    In a survey of more than 40,000 men, the quality most valued in a friend is the ability to keep confidences. Do you put things "in the vault" when someone shares something with you?

Be You - The greatest gift you can give to others is you—the *real* you. So, pull off your mask and be authentic!

Be observant – Pay attention. Sometimes you may just have to be quiet and listen.

Be available - You never know when you will be called on.
    Be considerate. Know when to press and when not to. Sometimes they just need you.

Be an example - Set an example. They are always watching you.

Be wise – Be discerning. Don't try fixing something that does not need to be fixed.

Be courageous - Know when to put it on the line. There are just times you have to call a timeout and just say that is just wrong.

Believe - Build them up; do not beat them up. Call out the best in them.

Repair Rifts - As rifts, misunderstandings arise. Tackle them head-on with gentle honesty.
    Never let a disagreement fester and damage what has been built.

Now develop a definition of a true friend

- Our definition was: they walk with you even when others don't.

WEEK 2

A REAL MAN

In this session we will talk about what is a real man and work toward a definition of a real man.

Bible Study: Psalms 15
Talk through the qualities found in Psalms 15

A Man Is...

Blameless

Righteous

Truthful

Does not slander

Kind to his neighbors (everyone)

Despises evil

Keeps promises

Giving not greedy

A man of integrity

A great promise - <u>unshakeable</u>

Now take the acronym A REAL MAN and come up with words that describe a real man - <u>here is ours</u>

A - Accountable - For his actions – No Blame Game

R - Respected - By Others
E - Example - Sets One
A - All In - Sold Out to God and His Family
L - Leads - Courageously

M - Mentors - Others
A - Accepts Responsibility - For His Actions
N - No - Understands Saying NO Is OK Sometime

Now Yours

A _____

R _____
E _____
A _____
L _____

M _____
A _____
N _____

Now use those words to come up with a definition of a real man. – <u>here is ours</u>

A Real Man Accepts Responsibility for his life. He is willing to stand up for what he believes no matter what; he also leads by example, and he is not afraid to be held accountable

Your Definition

_____
_____
_____
_____

LETTING GO OF THE PAST
GOD LOVES DO-OVERS

Wouldn't it be nice if you could just yell "do-over" and get a chance to do it again? If everything that happened in your life was written on a white board, wouldn't it be great if you could just walk up and erase the board, and make it clean again?

I've got good news for you. God specializes in do-overs.

- He can take a broken life and set it straight again.
- He can take a hopeless situation and give you hope.
- He can offer forgiveness to those who have messed up over and over.

WHY? - Because - He is the God of the do-over.

Bible Study: Isaiah 43:18-19 --- II Corinthians 5:17

Life Happens; we get too close to the edge.
Satan will take you farther than you want to go.
Satan will keep you longer than you want to stay.
Satan will cost you more than you want to pay.

God Just Loves Do-Overs
Definition of a Do-Over - A Fresh Start; New Beginning

II Corinthians 5:17 - "If anyone is in Christ Jesus, he is a new creation; the old has gone and the new has come."
The Message - "Anyone who is united with Christ gets a fresh start."

God Will . . .

- Take your past and exchange it for your future.
- Take your mess and exchange it for your message.

Formula To A Fresh Start

Isaiah 43:18-19 "Forget the former things; do not dwell on the past ¹⁹ See, I am doing a new thing.

S - Stop making excuses - I would like to let you in on a secret: God has heard all the good ones.
T - Take stock in your own life - God has a custom-created future just for you! Ephesians 2:10 – For we are God's masterpiece... You were born as an original. Don't die as a copy.

A - Action required - there comes a time in your life where you just have to take that bold step. Even you may not know where it will lead.

R - Refocus your thoughts

- Focus on what really is important to you
- Attention + Direction = Your Destination
- We all end up somewhere, but not many end up there on purpose.

T - Trust God - Trust that God can do what He says He can do, with whom He chooses, how He chooses. And you are HIS choice.

S - Stay focused on what really matters - Making one wrong choice in life can be devastating like a domino effect, but when you change what you are focusing on, everything can change in a moment. It happened in my life, and if God did it for me HE will do it for you too.

What It Will Take To Live Out Your Do-Over

You Will Have To...

1. Choose to see the big picture - David said in *Psalm 138:8* that God is more concerned about your future than your past, because your past is forgiven.

2. Choose to remember who you are - The real you is not what you and others see on the outside; it is what's on the inside.

3. Choose to see through the eyes of faith, not doubt - Faith will move mountains, but fear will create them.

4. Choose your words carefully - Be careful what you put behind I Am... - You really are God's BEST – you are HIS son

5. Choose to live in your present, not be trapped in the past - Be defined by what is ahead of you not what was behind you.

Never let your past become greater than your dreams.

WEEK 4

STORMS

In life, from time to time you will be hit with a storm. In this lesson, we will look at how to get through those storms.

Bible Study: Luke 8:22-25

Jesus got in the boat with them and said "Let's go to the other side." But a storm hit and they forgot what HE said and we do the same thing.

It's been said that everyone is either… - Talk Through

- **In a storm**
- **Just coming out of a storm**
- **Getting ready to go through a storm**

Where are you?

3 Causes of a Storm - Talk Through
1. **We cause them** – by our actions

2. **Others cause them** – actions of others

3. **God allows them** – to teach us

Could be an opportunity

To make you rest

Bring about a change

Storms – <u>Talk Through Points Below</u>

3 Things to do in a storm
1. Hold on - to what you know – Let's go you will make it

2. Learn – Ask "What can I learn from this storm?"

3. Stay – Until you know what to do

3 Things not to do in a storm
1. Panic – Do not allow fear to kick in

2. Quit – Stay the course – something will happen on the other side of the storm

3. Refuse help – God will send the right person to help you get through the storm

3 Things to do after the storm
1. Thank God – for getting you through the storm

2. Prepare for the next one – what did you learn?

3. Help someone - else get through their storm

Are you trying to get through a storm alone?

Is there someone in a storm that you know you should come along side of?

WEEK 5

WHAT IF I TOOK CONTROL OF MY WORDS?

You can't fully tame the tongue, but you can learn to control it.
It's not difficult to see the problems caused by the wrong use of words. You don't have to look far - more than likely only as far as your closest relationships.

Bible Study: Ephesians 4:29-31 --- Extra - James 3:1-6

Wrong words can destroy relationships.
There's a lie that we were all told as children. *Sticks and stones may break my bones but words will never hurt me.*
Words do hurt. Sticks and stones only hurt for a while, but words can hurt for a lifetime. After a while the words, or the lack of the words, take their toll on the relationship.

Wrong words can make a bad situation worse.
Whenever you continue to speak wrong words into a bad situation, you tend to fan the flame until it gets out of control.
So You Might Ask: WHAT GOOD WILL IT DO?

You'll become a better person. Someone said, "Change your thoughts and you'll change your world." BUT I say: "Change your words and you'll change yourself and those around you."

You'll build others up. Your words have the power to tear people down, or the power to build people up. Your words have the power to make people want to quit, or to encourage them to try one more time. It depends on how you use them.

HOW TO PUT IT INTO PRACTICE
1. Don't say everything you know.
You may know something about someone, but just because you know it, and just because it's true, doesn't mean you have to say it.
Ask yourself, "What good would it do if I told this?"

2. Use a filter.
This might sound suspiciously like a product endorsement, but have you ever used a Brita filter? It is supposed to take the bad stuff out of the water. Ephesians 4:29–31 gives us a filter for our words.

Wholesome words - unwholesome words are rotten fruit. I could tell you every day for twenty years that you are God's best, and in one day I could say one thing to you that would wipe out twenty years of investment. Be so careful with your words.

Appropriate words - speak to the needs of the moment.

Encouraging words - speak the best of others, building them up.

Truthful words - don't say something which is not true.

Transforming words - our words should build up.

Forgiving words - God has forgiven us; we need to forgive others.

Thankful words - do you thank people around you for the little things? Everyone needs to hear thankful words—including God.

_____ **words** - you fill in the blank.
As you think about your environment at home, at work, at church, what kind of words do you need to be speaking?

3. Don't say everything you think.
Some people believe they know a little bit more about every subject than anyone else. Solomon said (Proverbs 17:28) even a fool is thought wise if he keeps silent.
You don't have to say everything you think. So, remember to think first, speak second.

4. Don't repeat everything you hear.
The problem with repeating gossip is that it tends to get embellished as it is passed from person to person. This is why you need to think before you speak, and consider whether you should say anything at all.

Let me give you an awesome principle
Watch your thoughts ~ They become your words.
Watch your words ~ They become your actions.
Watch your actions ~ They become your habits.
Watch your habits ~ They become your character.

A key to overcoming bad habits is to start with your tongue, start with the words you say.

2 Words That Will Change Your Life.
<u>**Be purposeful**</u> ---- **Be purposeful in all you do.**
In Your parenting, marriage, forgiving - yourself and others, ministry, relationship with God, career, social media activity, education, financial life, life planning, relationship building, leadership. <u>**Be purposeful**</u>

WEEK 6

CONFLICT

In this session we will look at how to handle conflict in your life.

Bible Study: Matthew 18:15-17
Go Over Matthew 18:15-17 - Break it down and talk through these points

If you are in a conflict – There will be a time when you are in one. The difference is how you handle it.

You – That means you

Go – You be the bigger person here

To The Person – don't send a message - sometimes it just makes matters worse

In Private – Leave the crowd behind

Discuss The Problem – Discuss the one you are dealing with, not the ones from 10 years ago – feel free to set a time to do that

For The Purpose Of Reconciliation – Key here is relationships

Keep in mind the 101% rule - find the 1% you can agree on and give it 100%

6 Keys to Dealing with Conflict

1. Affirm The Relationship – Avoid the blame game here.
When you do A – I feel like B – example: When you don't call me back, I feel like I am not important

2. Keep Communication Open – Remember anger shuts the door

3. Defuse – Calm down – make a plan and set a time to talk to the other person – never do it when you are angry or hurt

4. Stay Focused On THE Conflict – Stick to the conflict at hand, not all the other junk that may get brought up

5. Listen Carefully – It may not be about you - you could have just been in the way. If it is you, use the 1st 4 keys

6. Forgive – Let it go move on

- **3 Promises that need to be made here**
- I promise, I will not bring this up again
- I promise, I will not hold it against you
- I promise, I will not let it hurt our relationship

What would it look like if you made something with these 3 Promises on it and hung it somewhere in your house?

Remember the 101% Rule

- **Find the 1% you can agree on and give it 100%**

ANGER

Anger is a great challenge for so many and in so many ways. Did you know the death rate is 7 times higher for people who have a tendency to just stay angry?

Anger is simply a natural emotional reaction to a displeasing situation or an event.

Bible Study: Ephesians 4:26-27
In here you will see 4 principles that will help us deal with anger.

Notice the command in Verse 26: In your anger do not sin. See, anger is not the problem – it becomes a problem when it is handled wrong.

Even Jesus got angry at injustice and wrong, but notice He did not sin in His anger – He just corrected the problem

1st Principle
Admit when you are angry – don't deny it – it will only get worse. Ask yourself, "Will it really change anything?"
    The key here is be careful of your words. Never forget that words are like a tube of tooth paste - once you squeeze it out it is hard to get it back in. If you don't talk it out, you will take it out.

2nd Principle
Understand It – Is it helpful anger or hurtful anger?
    Ask yourself two questions – What am I so angry about? And
    Why am I so angry? Find out what the root cause is, then you can deal with it. Is it coming from a hurt, a frustration, a fear? I have found in dealing with men most anger comes from a criticism or an injustice to them or someone close to them.

3rd Principle
Deal with it right away – Don't let the sun go down…
    If you do Satan has a foot hold and he can use that time to sometimes make matters worse. Look at what the verse says – Get over it. Deal with it because it can tear people apart.

4th Principle
4th Control it – do not allow anger to control you; don't allow anger to steal logical thinking from you.

Always fight fair
Fighting fair allows you to express your own needs while still respecting others.

Make the relationship your priority. Maintaining the relationship, rather than "winning" the argument, should always be your first priority. Be respectful of the other person and his or her viewpoint.

Focus on the present. Once you are in the heat of arguing, it's easy to start throwing the past into the mix. Focus on what you can do to solve the problem.

Choose your battles. Conflicts can be draining, so it's important to consider whether the issue is really worth your time and energy. If you pick your battles rather than fighting over every little thing, others will take you more seriously when you are upset.

Be willing to forgive. Resolving conflict is impossible if you're unwilling or unable to forgive.

Know when to let something go. If you can't come to an agreement, agree to disagree. It takes two people to keep an argument going. If a conflict is going nowhere, choose to move on.

4 Helpful Questions to Ask Yourself
1. What am I so angry about?
2. Why am I so angry?
3. Will it really change anything?
4. In the end will it really matter?

FORGIVENESS

They say unforgiveness is like you drinking poison and wanting the other person to die. As long as you hold on to unforgiveness, Satan has a tool he can use to mess with you.

Bible Study: See Scripture below
1. Our fellowship with God suffers when we refuse to release others from their sins against us (Matt. 6:14-15).

2. We should forgive over and over. In Matthew 18:22, Jesus tells Peter that he must forgive his brother "seventy times seven" times.

3. We must be willing to extend mercy towards those who sin against us, because God has forgiven each of us of so much (Matt.18:23-35).

4. We must deliberately turn away from anger and malice (Eph. 4:31-32).

Obstacles to Forgiveness – Add your own thoughts to each
1. **Lack of desire:**
2. **Rehearsing what happened:**
3. **Pride:**
4. **Fear:**
5. **Negative advice:**
6. **Partial forgiveness:**
7. **Relying on emotions:**
8. **Expecting quick results:**
9. **Justifying the other person's actions:**

Important Reminders
1. As a believer, you have the responsibility….
2. Forgiveness will not always be easy or quick…
3. Forgiving is difficult because it is unselfish…
4. You may never forgive if you wait until you "feel like it."
5. Remember, forgiveness doesn't always have to include going to the other person.

Dealing with the Anger that comes with not letting it go
1. Acknowledge that you have been totally forgiven.
2. Confess your anger to the Lord.
3. Recognize that unforgiveness is sin.
4. Ask God to forgive you.
5. Lay down the anger.

How to Know You Have Forgiven
1. The harsh emotions you've had towards others will be replaced by compassion.
2. You'll be able to accept others without feeling bitter.
3. You will feel thankful that God allowed the difficult experience.

Conclusion: You do not have to hold onto unforgiveness, bitterness, and resentment. Letting go is a choice. Is there someone you need to contact?

WEEK 9

ANXIETY AND STRESS

We live in a day where anxiety and stress seems to be at an all-time high. It simply means being pulled into two directions. Sad to say, many today are pulled in more than two directions.

Let's look at anxiety first

Bible Study: 1 Peter 5:7

4 Causes of Anxiety
1. **Feeling of inadequacy** – feeling like it's bigger than you, overwhelmed

2. **Try to control things you really have no control over** – some people or a situation

3. **Misplaces prioritized** – we try to do the wrong things at the wrong time.

3 Keys to time management
1. **Prioritize your time** – Important first
2. **Focus** – on the most important first (this is hard)
3. **Ignore all the distractions** – satan loves to distract you from doing the things that really matter

The **WIN** Method – What's Important Now

4. **Try to live tomorrow today** – this will steal your peace and your joy and can give you that overwhelmed feeling

The 'How' to getting rid of anxiety - I Peter 5:7
Vs. 6 - Cast All – Sounds way too simple. The sad part is we think we can handle it better than God can so we hold on to it.
Vs. 7 - And He will give you peace – what a promise

Stress
We get stressed out when we have too much going on. Stop for a moment and take a deep breath and ask yourself, "What are my top 3 priorities right now? What should they be?" Sometimes it's just as simple as re-focusing.

Bible Study: Luke 10:38-42
Martha loses her focus – she was focused on a good thing but the wrong thing, and it's the same with us.

Keys to Overcoming Stress
1. Recognize you are stressed – this is key because if you don't you will get even more stressed out as the day goes by

2. Take a breath – look at what's really going on are things in the right order?

3. Remove yourself – take a walk – get away from it – relax for a moment

4. Solve the small things first – so they don't become big things

5. Reflect - on Matthew 11:28-30

How can you make Matthew 11:28-30 short and simple so that when you get that feeling of being stressed out you can use it to help you get through it?

_____

_____

WEEK 10

DECISIONS

When we did this lesson, the discussion in the room was amazing. Keep it moving and the same will happen in your group.

Bible Study: Take time to look at each verse that is attached to each point.

7 Questions that will help you make better decisions

- Man, I wish someone had gone through these with me years ago.

1. What Biblical principle will help me with this decision?
Proverbs 3:5-6: This one is key to find something you can hang your hat on when you need to make a decision.

2. Do I have all the facts? Proverbs 18:13
Don't fall prey to wishful thinking

3. Is pressure pushing me? Proverbs 19:2
Be aware of today only or the once in a lifetime

4. What motives are pushing me? Proverbs 16:2
Check the blind spots – Good and Bad

5. How should the past affect this decision? Proverbs 26:11
Ask, "Am I digging another hole?"

6. Have I considered the outcome? Proverbs 27:12
Look at all the risk

7. Could or will this decision jeopardize my integrity? Proverbs 10:9

Ask yourself:

- Does this decision make sense?

- If so, why?

- If not, why not?

My Favorite:
What story do I want to tell when this is all over?

THE PATH TO A FALL

There are crossroads, back roads, peak experiences, mountains to climb, valleys of despair, deserts and oases, wildernesses and wastelands, rivers to cross, forks in the road, detours, dead ends, and the open road. They're all descriptive of places we've been. Wouldn't it be nice to know beforehand what how to avoid a fall?

Bible Study: Genesis 3:1-19 -- Luke 15:11-24

Notice when God shows up –Who did He call to? ADAM. Men, we need to take responsibly for our lives as well as our families lives

7 Steps to a Fall – (Talk through each of the 7 steps)

1. Deception – Making someone believe something that is not true Genesis 3:1-3

2. Distortion – Making things look different then they are Genesis 3:4-5

3. Decision – Never make a permanent decision in a temporary circumstance – Genesis 3:6a

4. Desire – Ask yourself, "When this is over, what story do I want to tell?" – Genesis 3:6b

5. Disobedience – Just doing the wrong thing - Genesis 3:6-7

6. Discovery – You will be found out – Don't play the name game here; if you did it, own up to it - Genesis 3:8-13

7. Destruction – A lot of destruction in our life can be avoided by just making better decisions – Genesis 3:14-19

When You Fall (we all have) **Never Forget...**

Psalms 37:23-24 - The LORD makes firm the steps of the one who delights in him; though he may stumble, he will not fall, for the LORD upholds him with his hand.

When you fall you have 3 choices
You can...

- **Let it destroy you** – destroy your hopes, dreams, life

- **Let it define you** – who you are – Men, you are HIS son.

- **Let it drive you** – to get back up – get in the game and live out all God has planned for your life

The Biggest Piece Of Advice I Can Give You Is:
Do NOT Wallow In It -- Learn from the Lost Son

The Path To A "Do-Over" - Luke 15:11-24
1. He came to his senses- vs. 17

2. He admitted his own need – vs. 17

3. He got up and returned to his Father - vs. 18-19

4. He was unconditionally accepted by his Father - vs. 20

5. The Father celebrated His son's return – vs. 21-23

6. The son started life all over again – vs. 24

God will take your mess and exchange it for your message.
Talk about a part of your life here

WEEK 12

DON'T LET THE ENEMY LOOT YOUR LIFE

In life, satan (I never capitalize satan - that gives him too much credit) will use all kinds of things to try to steal from you the life God intended you to live. In this session, over the years there are 9 things that keep coming up over and over again, so let's deal with them here.

Bible Study: Take time to look at each verse that is attached to each point.

An 86 year old man once said, "I regret the things I didn't do far more than the things I did."

If you were to die tomorrow, what would be your biggest regret?

John 10:10 – 10: The thief comes only to steal and kill and destroy; **(BUT)** I have come that they **(YOU)** may have life, and have it to the full.

1. Your uniqueness. *(Ephesians 2:10)*

- You were born an original. DON'T die a copy!

2. Your choice to let go of the past *(2 Corinthians 5:17)*

- Scars remind you of where you have been, not where you are headed.

3. Your choice to forgive *(Ephesians 4:32)*

- Not forgiving someone is like drinking poison and expecting the other person to die. Forgiveness is a gift you give to yourself

4. Your Attitude *(Colossians 4:17)*

- Something no one can take away from you is how you choose to respond in any given circumstance.

5. Your Time *(Colossians 3:23)*

- Become the Master of Your Time - What you do today must be important because you are exchanging a day of your life for it.

6. Your Courage to Overcome Fear of <u>BLANK</u> *(Joshua 1:11)*

- Your greatest stories will come from overcoming your greatest struggles.

7. Your passion *(Jeremiah 29:11)*

- Your passion is the little voice inside that whispers "YES" when it seems like the whole world is shouting impossible.

8. Life Experiences *(Hebrews 11)*

- Life will teach you some amazing lessons that you can use to impact the lives of others.

9. Your ability to leave a legacy *(2 Timothy 4:7)*

- The measure of your life will not be in what you accumulate, but in what you give away. How do you want to be remembered?

Brooks Robinson said, "Every day we serve as a role model – good or bad."

Some Legacies Men Want To Leave Behind
(These are from some of the men) -- <u>Legacy session week 22</u>

1. A Legacy of a Role Mode
2. A Legacy of Excellence
3. A Legacy of Encouragement
4. A Legacy of What a Real Man Looks Like
5. A Legacy of _____

Add your thoughts and ask the men to add their thoughts

YOUR WIFE NEEDS A HERO - AND IT'S YOU

What makes a hero? Superman's super human strength isn't natural. Batman's fortune was inherited. Spiderman is genetically mutated. These super human powers aren't physically achievable. Even Iron Man is still a fictional character. Just putting on the suit isn't enough. It's their character. Their deep care and compassion for their cities, families and friends, along with some special abilities, is what makes them heroes. Your wife is no different. Your actions can make you her hero.

Bible Study: Ephesians 5:25

1. Be there for her. If she's had a bad day, listen, and make her smile. Be there. Be involved.

2. Romance your wife. Love your wife and remind her why you fell in love in the first place. Let your wife know that she is lovely; her heart needs to hear that.

3. Set the example as the spiritual leader in your house. Be the spiritual leader in your household for your wife and your kids. Talk about the Lord, pray together, take the family to church, make Him your focus.

4. Support her. Everyone faces battles. You are her husband. Be there to support your wife when she faces her battles. You cannot always fight them for her, but you can stand by her. That will make you the hero.

5. Listen. As a husband, you will be her shoulder to cry on, her man to hug. She shares these things with you because she loves you.

6. Spend time together. Doing things you enjoy together, appreciating one another's company, sharing moments and memories as couple and as a family allows you the golden opportunity to be your wife's hero.

7. Pay attention to detail. Try to pay attention to little details. Notice new haircuts, compliment new clothes, and learn facial expressions. Remember important occasions such as anniversaries and holidays. Plan ahead for them in order to make reservations or find the perfect gift. This shows her you care and you will be a hero.

8. Give her a break. Once you and your wife have children, the dynamics change some. Your wife will occasionally just need a break and a chance to escape from everything. Volunteer to watch the kids, give her time to be free. Or arrange a sitter so the two of you have a chance to get away together for a date night. - *Date Nights Are Key*

9. Commit to your wife. It is not enough in a marriage to love your wife. You need to commit to her to demonstrate that love. The most important thing is to be there; be present. When things get hard in life or your marriage, do not run. Work through things together. Overcoming obstacles together will strengthen your marriage. Heroes don't become heroes by cowering from life's problems. They conquer them.

10. Appreciate her. Take note of all the little things that she does and thank her for doing them. Tell her know how important she is to you. Most importantly, thank God for blessing you with a woman to love for the rest of your life.

Which one do you need to work on today?

What are you taking from this lesson you will apply when you get home?

<u>Closing - Men the cape is optional – begin a hero is not</u>

WEEK 14

7 TIPS FOR COMMUNICATION IN MARRIAGE

I have learned in my marriage that most of MY problems come from me not listening or trying to fix things that really don't need to be fixed. Can you relate?

Bible Study: A Strange Verse for Communication, BUT so true **Ecclesiastes 3:3 & 7b** - A Time for Everything - 3 There is a time for everything, <u>7b - a time to be silent and a time to speak,</u>

Be a good listener – You can never expect to grow in your communication until you learn to truly hear one another.

Timing is important – Don't try to address major issues when the other party is distracted. Set aside time to address important topics.

Never criticize the person – You can address actions, but when you attack the person, defenses rise and communication fails.

Be willing to give each other credit for differences
Men can't talk to wives as they talk to their guy friends.
    Ladies, if they want the guy to understand something… They must say it in a language you understand… men understand facts…men don't read subtleties or between the lines… <u>Agree/or Not & Why</u>

Keep emotions under control – When girls start shedding tears and men's anger rises, communication is hindered. Wait until the intense emotion passes, then address the issue. <u>Pause Men</u>

Prompt resolutions – Don't let issues linger too long. Don't let the sun go down on your anger. The longer an issue lingers, the harder it is to address.

Be willing to humble yourself and forgive – Marriage is hard; people make mistakes; marriage must be free flowing with grace.

What would you add to the list?

What has improved the communication in your marriage?

CHILDREN

Tips for parents for healthy discipline

Helping us understand the reason behind proper discipline.

Bible Study: Proverbs 29:17 says, "Discipline your son, and he will give you peace; he will bring delight to your soul."

Never discipline in anger. You will say things you do not mean and do things you should not do. Discipline done is anger is rarely productive and usually harmful long-term. Remember these 3-steps; Stop/Think/Proceed.

Be consistent in your discipline plan. It will mean nothing to the child otherwise. Don't just re-act; at the same time, do not overkill a minor incident or ignore a major occurrence.

Differentiate discipline for each child. Every child is different, so discipline in a way that works best for the child.

Do not make threats with which you are unwilling to follow through. Your child will catch on to that real quick.

Always discipline the child for results. Discipline in its concept is not necessarily pleasant, but it reaps a reward if done right. Hebrews 12:11 says, "No discipline seems pleasant at the time, but painful. Later on, however, it produces a harvest of righteousness and peace for those who have been trained by it."

Discipline should never teach children that they are unloved. Actually, if done right, it should reinforce the love a parent has for the child.

5 key words to keep in mind
These are principles that can greatly increase your success as a dad.

Plan – We have a plan for most other areas of our life other than for our family. Plan a strategy for raising children the way you want them to go.

Protect – It is critically important to protect your relationship with the child, so that you can have influence in their life. This is not accomplished by giving them what they want, but by gently balancing discipline with love.

Control – The time to gain control over a child's actions are when they are young and then a gradual release of authority is given to them, as they get older. Too many parents allow too much freedom early and then try to get control back when the child tries to be a rebellious teenager. I think it should be the opposite.

Invest – Children require an intentional investment of time and energy from you. Having children who grow up well does not usually just happen, but it is as a result of the right investment of your time.

Model – You cannot expect children to learn principles you are not willing to model for them. Children should not be held to higher standards than you hold yourself.

DAD THEY ARE WATCHING YOU!
Your children are watching you:
To see how dedicated we are to the things we say we believe in.
To see how patient we are with others.
To see how we behave when no one else is around but them.
To see how we treat our spouse.
To see how deeply we care for the hurts of others.
To see how committed our walk is with Christ.
To see if we tell the truth.

WORK

Becoming the Christian Man at Work that God Wants You to Be

If someone were to ask the people you work with if you were a Christian, what would they say?

Bible Study: Colossians 3:23 and 1 John 2:6 – Your Thoughts

Colossians 3:23 -

1 John 2:6 -

What is God's purpose and design for a man at work?

Are you at a job where He wants to use you?

Are you over working, under working or are you passive?

Are you working so much you are missing time with your family?

If your perception of yourself is your work and your position, who are you if you lose your work?
    Movie: The Company Man: A Man loses his high paying job and has trouble with his "real" significance to his friends and his family.

Have you ever lost a job?

How did you feel? - What did you do?

Did you have someone to go to for prayer or just show up and talk with you?

Would you be there for a fellow professional/worker if they lost their job?

Our Example
1 John 2:6 "Whoever says that he abides in Jesus ought to walk in the same way in which Jesus walked."

Do your fellow workers see examples of Christ in your integrity, your language, or respect to your bosses/managers? If not what can you do to change it?

What if someone said: "You have a great attitude at work how do you do it." What would you tell them?

- <u>Ask them for their thoughts before you go over the points below</u>

6 Keys for a Man at Work
Performance at work - strive for excellence as an example because it is required of us.

Being dependable - If your son or daughter were to go to work in the same place where you work, what would they hear about you from your fellow workers?

Take responsibility for actions - Be responsible for your thoughts, feelings, words, and actions. "Own" the choices you make and the results that follow.

Integrity - Be sincere and real. Living in integrity means that everything we say and everything we do are true reflections of what we value, what's important to us.

Speak honestly and kindly - Think before you speak. Words are powerful! They have the power to uplift and enlighten or put down.
A few cutting words spoken in a moment of anger can affect us and others for a long time, perhaps even a lifetime. Keep in mind, what we say to others—and to ourselves—can have a huge impact

Understand you will get the challenging jobs at work - Because they can trust you. Example: My father as a welder in the shipyard. He was asked to be a welder on the nuclear reactors when they first were used on ships. - I am very proud of my dad.

IT'S YOUR TIME

Sometimes in life we wonder what's next, and that is where Joshua was. Moses had died, all the hopes and dreams seem gone, and then one day God shows up and tells Joshua, "Moses my servant is dead. Now get ready."

Have you been waiting on something and God has been trying to get you to move?

Bible Study: Joshua 1: 1-8
Joshua wrestling with fear – Moses was dead - Now What?
   God shows up and tells Joshua: It's Your Time

1. It's NOW your time – Waited 45 years – AT JUST the RIGHT Time, God shows up

- even though Moses was dead God's purpose was still alive.

2. The assignment is clear - God's message was clear

- His instructions were very explicit

3. You have to move - what is God saying that you need to do?

- Ps 24:1 the earth is the Lord's and everything in it...
- God had given them the land, BUT now they had to move to get it. The same land Joshua explored 38 years earlier (Numbers 13:1-16)

4. You have to trust God is WITH you. - TODAY
When God gives a command He always accompanies it with a promise. Look at the words I will never leave you....
God never walks out on a promise
    It has to be about HIM - The heat is not on you to get it done; it's on God.

5. Be Strong and courageous - *very courageous* - God did not ask Joshua anything - He told him to be strong. The way you become courageous is step into one victory at a time.

- **God Memories -** God memories help us to remember what is really important in life --- **Psalm 143:5** - "I remember the days of long ago; I mediate on all your works and consider what your hands have done"

6. Success is found in MY WORD
God speaks when what HE has already said is honored
    To be ... successful - Joshua was to do three things with regard to the Scriptures:

(a) The Law was not to depart from his mouth; he was to hold on to it (Ps 1:1-3)
(b) He was to meditate on it day and night, to think about it
    (Ps. 1:2; 119:97)
(c) He was to obey its commands fully and to act by it
    (James 1:22-25)

God gave Joshua 3 things he could hold on to:

- **His promise**
- **His power**
- **His presence**

He gives the same things to us.

UNPACKING YOUR LUNCH

God has given every man a lunch (gifts and talent) to use to impact people around him. In this lesson we will look at the story of a little boy that gave his 5 loaves and 2 fish to Jesus and a miracle happened. What do you have that God wants to use?

Bible Study: John 6:1-15

YOUR "LUNCH" CAN BE DEFINED AS: Your God-given potential

Four Things Make Up Your Lunch
Your Time - 86,400 sec. – 1440 min.
Your Talent - how God has gifted you
Your Treasure - what you hold valuable
Your Touch - pain, mistakes

Principle: God calls you to partner with Him on a mission that is bigger than you are.

The number one reason many never Unpack Their Lunch is <u>**FEAR**</u> – this is the answer I get 80% of the time

Unpacking Your Lunch
Unpacking can be defined as: How God wants you to deploy your God-given potential.

1. **It originates from the heart of God.** Jesus had compassion

2. **Be ready when God calls upon you.** You feed them

3. **It seeks to meet a God-size need.** Impacting people

4. **It is not conditional to you.** God wants to use you

5. You must see through the eyes of your heart, not your head. What is God putting in your heart that is causing it to break?

6. It seeks to meet the unmet need, not just fix the problem.
Jesus wanted to teach them, not just fix them

7. The results are not based on our resources but God's.
Jesus just wants you to give HIM your lunch - He will do the rest

8. Don't let anyone despise what you have to offer.
They asked, "What is this among so many?" We do the same thing, then sad to say we do nothing.

9. Give thanks for what God is going to do. For what God is going to do

10. A little miracle goes a long way. 12 baskets left over

Keys To Unpacking Your Lunch
It begins with a concern - The Big question to ask is, will my lunch impact the lives of others?

The WHAT always precedes the HOW.
You will always know what God has put in your heart to do, long before you know the how.

Your Lunch + Your Faith = God's Miracle
Question: What is God laying on your heart that could have only come from HIM?

_____

Questions
Is there something specific that ignites your passion?

What would you like to be remembered for?

If you had unlimited resources and complete freedom to fail, what would you attempt for God?

Principle: God calls you to be on mission with Him right where you are; starting now.

DISCOVERING YOUR PURPOSE

God has put something amazing inside of you and HE is waiting for you to value it enough to live it out.

Bible Study: Proverbs 29:18 – Also read it in The Message

3 Things That Will Stop You

1. Voices: There will always be plenty of people willing to tell you why you can't

2. Fear: Fear will always create mountains, BUT faith can move them

3. Interruptions: Allowing things to stop us or slow us down

4 Things To Remember

1. Your entire life has been leading up to your purpose.

2. The how is never a problem for God, just us.

3. You will be stretched.

4. Purpose can never be taken away, unless you allow it.

3 Things A Purpose Will Do

- A purpose evokes passion
- A purpose provides motivation
- A purpose gives direction

A God-given Purpose
Will…

open your eyes – to see what God sees

open new doors – then you will have to walk through them

provide a push – in some cases it may be a kick

bring out our best – it's already inside of you

bring things into focus – you start to see things clearly

give significance to what seems to be trivial

A PAL To Finding Your Purpose

Passion - what burns inside of you

Abilities - gifting, talents

Life – life experiences

The WHAT always precedes the HOW
You will always know what God has put in your heart to do, long before you know the how.

The Journey To Your Purpose
You see it - Something stirs you. It keeps you up at nights and wakes you up early.

You doubt it – Satan will provide quitting points. Press on: don't put limits on God.

7 Ways To See If It's A God Thing Or Your Thing
1. They say it can't be done.
2. You feel you aren't qualified.
3. There aren't enough resources.
4. It makes no rational sense.
5. People call it (or you) crazy.
6. It will not let go of you.
7. It would impact the lives of others.

You catch it - This is where it drives you

You own it - You live it out

Living Out Your Purpose
Start where you are. - When a God-given opportunity comes along, it is God's gift to you; what you do with it is your gift to Him

Use what you have. - How God has gifted you will be a good indication of the direction God is going to take you

Do what you can do. - When God shows your purpose, He goes to work behind the scene
Your purpose always leads you in the direction of something God is concerned about.

<u>**Handout For Week 20 Lesson -- Next Page**</u>

DISCOVERING YOUR PURPOSE

The following is a list of questions that can assist you in discovering your purpose. They are meant as a guide to help you in defining your personal mission statement.

Instructions:
1. Please answer using something other than family - that should be a given.
2. Take out a few sheets of loose paper and a pen.
3. Find a place where you will not be interrupted. Turn off your cell phone.
4. Write the answers to each question down - Without editing.
5. Write the first thing that pops into your head.
6. Write out your answers without thinking.
7. Write quickly. Less than 60 seconds a question. Preferably 30 seconds.
8. Be honest. Nobody will read it. It's important to write it down.
9. Enjoy the moments that make you smile as write.

Questions:
1. What makes you smile? (activities, people, events, hobbies, projects, etc.)

2. What are your favorite things to do now? How about the past?

3. What activities make you lose track of time?

4. Who inspires you most? Name 3 people. (family, friends, authors, leaders, etc.) Which 1 or 2 qualities inspire you in each person?

5. What are you naturally good at? (skills, abilities, gifts, etc.)

6. What do people typically ask you for help in?

7. If you had to teach something, what would you teach?

8. What were 2 challenges, difficulties and hardships you've overcome?

9. If you had one message to preach, what would it be about?

10. If you had unlimited resources and complete freedom to fail, what would you attempt for God?

Notice anything that comes up over and over again? List them now.
Example: educate, accomplish, empower, encourage, improve, help, give, guide, inspire, integrate, motivate, nurture, organize, produce, promote, spread, share, satisfy, understand, teach, write, etc.

_____

_____

What stirred you the most will be a good indication on your purpose.

Write the words or like words you see over and over again.

_____

_____

Example: cooking, serving, feeding people.

Your purpose is:

_____

Example: Starting a ministry that serves meals to people in need.

WEEK 21

GOD'S NOW MOMENTS

Every day you are perfectly positioned in the place you are in for God to use you to touch the life of someone else. BUT sad to say we are busy with other things. A good friend told me one day you will never look into the eyes of someone Jesus does not love. We can change this world by touching one life at a time.

Bible Study: Acts 3: 1-9

Someone wrote: "Now Moments are as numerous as the stars in the sky and the sands in the sea, and any of them could prove to be a significant moment. Within those now moments, a handful will become a defining moment in your life. However mundane a now moment may appear, the miraculous may wait to be unwrapped within it. Yet the only now moment that you must take responsibility for is the one in front of you. This is your moment!"

God is calling you to a life-changing journey alongside him.

3 Things We Know About Now Moments

1. Seldom find their way onto your calendar

- they happen while going through life

2. Have a mind of their own

- they don't care about interrupting you

3. Can be missed

- because of our busyness

Principle: God is always looking for ways to use you.

- Because you can have affect on the people God puts around you

Are You Ready? - Acts 3:1-9

God Shows UP When Men...

1. **Do the right thing vs. 1**

2. **Are willing to be interrupted vs. 3**

3. **Pay attention to others vs. 4**

4. **Are willing to offer hope vs. 5**

5. **Are willing to use what they have vs. 6**

6. **Understand it is not about you BUT God vs. 6-7**

7. **Understand touching one could impact many vs. 9**

When facing your Now Moment a few things to remember?

- **The Now is up to God** – be ready when HE calls

- **Ask God to help you find the Now in them**

- **Seizing is your choice** – it's up to you don't miss it

- **Don't get stuck in the past** – allow God to use your past to impact someone's life

The Results Of Your Now Moments

- The lost find direction

- The helpless find help

- The weary find new strength

- The hurting find healing

LIVING TO LEAVE A LEGACY

"Carve your name on hearts, not tombstones. A legacy is etched into the minds of others and the stories they share about you."

It's been said that everyone dies twice - once when you breathe your last breath and then when your name is mentioned for the last time.

Here is my definition; Legacies are rare and special gifts, from one person to another, from one generation to the next.

Someone did a research project with people over the age of 90. They asked: "As you look back on your life, what do you wish you had done differently?"

Three answers seem to come up over and over:
1) they wished they had lived out their dream
2) they wished they had spent more time with family
3) they wished they had done more to leave a legacy

Men, YOU have to Live to Leave a Legacy
Bible Study: Paul is coming to the end of his life and he makes an awesome statement in 2 Timothy 4:7 where he tells us what it will take to leave a legacy. He says – "I have fought the good fight; I have finished the race; I have kept the faith"

Four Lies Satan Wants You To Believe:
1. You Can Leave A Great Legacy Without Seeking God's Direction
So many people try to do it all on their own. Thinking that money, fame, status or possessions are all that is necessary to make you happy and to build a great life. It is impossible to leave a Godly legacy in your life and with your family without God in the center.

2. You Must Have It All Together To Leave A Great Legacy
In His Word, God gives us example after example of the weak or the poor doing mighty things. How is this possible? Because God has and will give you everything you will ever need at just the right time.

3. Your Mistakes Will End Any Chance For A Great Legacy
Satan tells us that we've made too many mistakes, we've lived the wrong way, we've lived in sin for too long - how can we leave a legacy? Don't let satan fool you into thinking that you've disqualified yourself from becoming what God wants you to become.

4. Leaving A Great Legacy Is Really Not That Important
Don't get so busy that we forget about what's important. Don't get so involved in your careers, in your pursuits, in your interests and hobbies that you get stuck in a rut. You know, that place where one day you look back and wonder where life went.

Five Legacies We Need To Leave
1. A Legacy of A Role Mode
You serve as a role model for your wife, your children, your friends and your colleagues.

Spend time with people you love. Show your family and friends that you truly do enjoy their company by spending time with them.

2. A Legacy of Excellence
To leave a legacy of excellence, strive to be your best every day. As you strive for excellence you inspire excellence in others. One person in pursuit of excellence raises the standards and behaviors of everyone around them.

3. A Legacy of Encouragement
You have a choice: you can lift others up or bring them down. Twenty years from now when people think of you, what do you want them to remember?

4. A Legacy of Purpose
To leave a legacy of purpose, make your life about something bigger than you.

While you're not going to live forever, you can live on through the legacy you leave and the positive impact you make in the world.

5. A Legacy of _____. Share your thoughts

The way you live your life is your greatest legacy, and since you only have one life to give, give all you have.

Closing - Just before a NCAA Championship football game, a coach wanted to encourage his players to step up to another level.

In his pre-game speech, he asked a powerful question: "What do you want to be remembered for? Do you want to be remembered as champions or losers?" Notice the simple question he asked – What do you want your legacy to be?

So let me ask you...
Will you live your life - With NO regrets - With NO retreats - With NO reserves

What kind of legacy will you leave? - Start on it today.

WHAT KIND OF MAN WAS JOSEPH?

When you read through the Gospels, very little is said about Joseph. We know that he was a man who worked in the building trades. We hear him mentioned at Jesus' birth, during Jesus' years as a young child, and briefly when Jesus was 12 years old. After that, we see nothing more about him. But his life spoke volumes.

Joseph was a man who had decided that he would do things the right way.
    The right way to Joseph was the way God had said things should be.

Bible Study: MATTHEW 1:18-25

Let us strive to have a heart like Joseph.
1. Joseph had a heart that was Pliable and Teachable

2. Joseph had a heart that was filled with Love and Compassion

3. Joseph had a heart of Obedience to the Word of the Lord

4. Joseph had a heart Beyond Reproach

5. Joseph a man of Integrity

6. Joseph a man of Character

7. Joseph a man of Compassion

Joseph was a man that was willing to listen, teachable, filled with love and compassion, willing to walk in obedience to the Word of God. Joseph was a man willing to do the right thing - the right way.

How about you?

THOUGHTS TO USE

TELLING YOUR STORY

Every day God is writing a story with your life, and that story can impact many over a lifetime.

If you had one day to put your story on a billboard where thousands of people pass by it, what would it say?

If you got on an elevator with someone and they asked you to tell them your story, what would you tell them?

3 Reasons Your Story Is Important
1. Your story can offer hope
2. Your story can help you connect
3. Your story can leave a mark

John Maxwell said that if you want to make a difference, do something that can make a difference at the time it can make a difference--tell your story.

3 Problems Kick In When We Start To Tell Our Story
1. We are not prepared, so we ramble on
2. Fear kicks in - what will they think
3. My story doesn't matter

8 Keys To Telling Your Story
1. Based it on your life – personal
2. Keep it simple
3. Keep it short - 30 sec. to 2 minutes
4. Build it around a singular point
5. Make it relevant – be real
6. Has to roll off of your tongue
7. Leave them with a take-away
8. When you finish – stop talking

The Prep Of Your Story

1. Pick your message
2. Build your story around these points

   - The problem - The change - The solution
   - Me - God - We

3. Write down your thoughts
4. Decide if it's going to be a 30 sec. - 60 sec. - 90 sec. or 2 minute story
5. Cut out the fluff – focus on the details
6. Short powerful sentences will make it easier to memorize it
7. Add the take-away
8. Work on the ending, so you can stop talking and let it stir in their heart

Thoughts For Your Story

Four of My Favorites

1. 30 second story – one word - your story – before God was in your life (rejected) – after God came into your life (called)

2. 60 second story – What is the biggest life lesson you have learned to date?

3. 30 second - 60 second story – Where were you? Where are you now and where are you headed with your life?

4. 60 second - 2 minute story – How bad did it get and how awesome God made it

Sample: I could not listen to the crowd; I found out there will always be plenty of people willing to tell me who they thought I should be or what I should become. One day a friend came along and told me God had put something amazing inside of me and HE was waiting for me to value it enough to live it out. Then he told me I was born an original; don't die a copy.

Extra Sessions

For Men

Helping Men Prepare For Life's Battles

PRAYER MADE SIMPLE

Prayer is simply talking to God—and the most important thing I can say about this is that God wants you to talk to Him!

God has also made it possible for us to communicate with Him through prayer. He speaks to us through His Word, the Bible. Therefore, the more we pray and read His Word, the deeper our relationship will grow with Him.

The Bible Study: **Matthew 6: 9-13**

A simple guide to prayer can be remembered by the word ACTS.

A stands for *adoration* in which we praise and speak well of God. - Our Father...

C is *confession* in which we admit our faults and our need for God's grace. - Forgive us...

T is *thanksgiving* in which we express gratitude for God's blessings in our lives. - For your daily...

S stands for *supplication* in which we ask God for the help and blessings we need. - And lead us...

* Remember As You Pray, It Is Simply Talking With God As You Would A Close Friend.

2 Keys

Ask God to help you make time for regular prayer. God gives wisdom to those who ask (Jas. 1:5), and He will help you as you ask Him. Jesus knew what it was like to have many things to do and a lot of demands on Him, yet He found time to pray (Mk. 6:30–46).

He knows our challenges and will help us as we come before Him (Heb. 4:14–16 - Put a time into your schedule or planner. If you treat prayer like an important meeting or appointment then you'll be much more likely to keep it.

Stick with it? Like going to the gym, the "muscles" of prayer don't develop overnight. Every new habit takes time to develop, so be disciplined and "don't despise the day of small beginnings" (Zech. 4:10). If it would help you to stay more consistent in prayer, why not ask someone to keep you accountable to your schedule?

A DAILY QUIET TIME OR BIBLE STUDY

I often encounter people who want to begin a daily quiet time, but they aren't sure how. It really isn't as complicated as we often make it out to be.

Here are 5 easy steps to begin a daily quiet time:

Place - Pick a definite place where you'll be every day for your quiet time. Obviously if you travel frequently this is more difficult, but the more routine you can make this the better. It should be as free of distractions as possible. This place will soon become very comfortable to you.

Schedule Time - Pick a reasonable amount of time and put it on your schedule. Start with 15 minutes, maybe even 10. The key at this point is consistency, so make sure you don't burden yourself with something you will not do. By the way, it most likely will seem like a sacrifice at first, but keep the objective in mind.

Format - Decide basically how you will structure your quiet time. If developing prayer is your goal, then certainly choose to spend more time in prayer. If Bible knowledge is your goal, then you may want to choose a reading plan. You can change the format over time and do combinations of each of these.

Activities – Decide what you will specifically do in your time. Will you do a Bible study or simply read Scripture and Pray? If your time is 15 minutes, for example, you could spend 6 minutes reading the Bible; 3 minutes talking to God; 2 minutes in silence, asking God to speak to you; and 4 minutes writing your thoughts at the time. The key is that you decide before you start what you are going to do during this time.

Discipline – Commit to doing something consistently for at least 30 days. Every day - without exception - do it, whether you "feel" like it or not. If you miss the exact time, make it up later in the day. Habits and lifestyles form this way and you'll need this discipline, because as soon as you attempt this dozens of obstacles will stand in your way. Over time, it becomes a habit that is easily repeated. Even better, it will soon become the best and most productive part of your day.

See The Post-It Note Bible Study (it is very successful for us)

Bible Study: 2 Timothy 3:16-17 – Talk Through Points Below

Paul tells Timothy that **all Scripture is God-breathed** "inspired", and is "useful" for every aspect of Timothy's ministry.
- **teaching – doctrine** - (instructing believers in God's truths)
- **rebuking – conviction** - (1 Tim. 5:20; 2 Tim. 4:2)
- **correcting – setting right** - those in error (2 Tim. 2:25; 4:2)
- **training – instruction** - ("child-training")

in righteousness (guiding new believers in God's ways)
the man of God (who must provide spiritual leadership to others)
is equipped ("for all situations" or "mature.")
for every good work (2:21).

Give the men this verse for the week. Find out which one works for them.

1 Corinthians 16:13:14 - Be on your guard; stand firm in the faith; be courageous; be strong. Do everything in love.

Post-It Note Bible Study For Men (See next page)

Scripture: _____ **Chapter:** _____ **Verses:** ____ - ____

Day 1 - _____
_____

Day 2 - _____
_____

Day 3 - _____
_____

Recap day 1-3 and write down the Big Idea you get from the verses above.
_____
_____

How can I apply it in my life: _____
_____

Another Simple Tool For Bible Study

Three Basic Steps

- **Observation:** What does it say? (facts)
- **Interpretation:** What does it mean? (lessons)
- **Application:** How does the meaning apply to me? (listen)

Post-It Note Bible Study For Men

Scripture: _____ Chapter: _____ Verses: ___ - ___

Day 1 - _____

Day 2 - _____

Day 3 - _____

Recap day 1-3 and write down the Big Idea you get from them.

_____

How can I apply it in my life? _____

_____

Four Questions To Ask Yourself

Scripture: _____ **Chapter:** _____ **Verse:** ___ - ___

You may not find all of the questions in every verse.
1. What does verse say to me right now?

2. Is there an example for me to follow?

3. Is there something I need to avoid?

4. Is there a something to apply to my life?

Made in the USA
Middletown, DE
19 March 2016